Clean Energy

Written by Kerrie Shanahan

Flying Start
to Literacy®

Contents

Introduction

Energy is essential to all of us. It allows us to have homes with lights, it keeps us warm and it keeps us cool, and it is used to cook our food. We can travel in cars, boats and aeroplanes. We can communicate instantly with people all around the world.

Everything and everybody in our world uses energy. The simplest way to describe energy is to say that it is the ability to do work.

Almost all energy on Earth comes from the sun, our closest star. The sun has been producing energy for billions of years and it is expected that it will continue to do so for the next five billion years.

The sun's energy
It is calculated that in only 71 minutes the Earth receives enough solar energy from the sun to provide for the energy needs of the entire population of the world for one year.

Chapter 1

Fossil fuels and energy

Electricity is the form of energy that we use most. We need electricity to power our world – we need it for light, warmth, communication and transport, as well as countless other things in our lives.

In most countries, electricity is made from burning coal, oil or gas. These are fossil fuels. Today, fossil fuels are the cheapest and most commonly used way to produce energy. Fossil fuels take millions of years to form. They are found deep below the surface of the Earth.

How are fossil fuels made?

Over time, the heat of the Earth and the weight and pressure of soil and rocks turns the remains of dead plants and animals into fossil fuels – coal, oil and gas.

There are problems with using fossil fuels. As the population of the world grows, our need for energy also grows. In the future, we will need even more energy than we are using now.

Once we have used all of the fossil fuels on Earth, they will be gone forever. They are non-renewable energy sources.

Also, when we make and use energy from fossil fuels, dangerous gases can be released into the air. This creates pollution and is changing the climate of our planet.

These problems have caused many people to look for other resources that can be used to create energy – resources that will not run out and do not pollute the Earth.

A coal power station burning fossil fuels to produce electricity

Are there ways to make and use energy that do not harm the planet?

Renewable energy is the way of the future. It cannot be depleted like fossil fuels and it doesn't produce harmful pollution. People are continuing to explore new ideas that use clean, renewable energy.

Hydroelectricity ▶

The energy from water in fast-flowing rivers is captured and turned into electricity known as hydroelectricity.

◀ Geothermal energy

Heat from deep in the Earth is used to make geothermal energy.

◀ Wind energy

Wind farms harness the power of the wind.

Wave power ▶

The tides of the ocean and the movement of the ocean's waves are used to create power.

◀ Solar energy

Solar energy is produced by the sun. Solar energy will not run out for the next five billion years!

9

Solar energy

Of all the sources of renewable energy, solar energy can most easily be turned into electricity. Because of this, solar power can be used by individual people living in towns and cities. You cannot build a large wind farm in your yard to create energy, but you can put solar cells on your roof and make electricity to use in your home.

The houses in this neighbourhood in Freiburg, Germany, have solar panels on their roofs. They can make so much electricity from the sun in summer that they sell it back to the power companies.

There is a problem with solar power. At night, there is no sunshine, and on cloudy days, the amount of solar energy generated is limited. But storage batteries that can be used in the home have been created. These batteries store energy so that it can be used when needed, at nighttime or when there is no sun.

In the near future, these batteries will become more efficient and less expensive so that many more people will be able to use them.

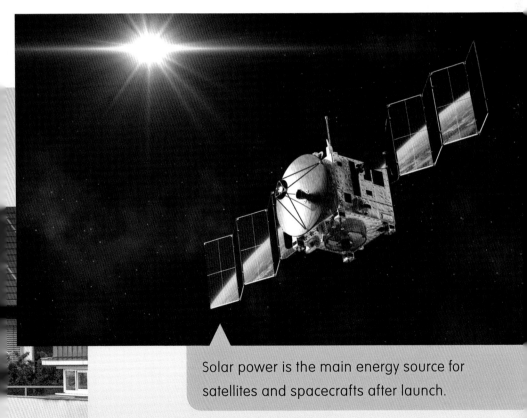

Solar power is the main energy source for satellites and spacecrafts after launch.

Chapter 2

A clean, green school

Think of all the energy your school uses. Computers, lights, heating, cooling and charging devices are just some of the many ways we use energy every day. Wouldn't it be great if the electricity used by your school came from a renewable energy source? That would really help the environment.

Well, for one Australian primary school, this is the case. Chewton Primary School near Castlemaine in Victoria is now partly powered by solar power.

But it hasn't always been this way. Being an older building, the school wasn't very energy efficient and a lot of electricity was being used and wasted. And the electricity was made using fossil fuels. The students and staff wanted to use a clean energy source. So, they decided to install solar panels.

Chewton Primary School
Chewton Primary School was opened in 1870. The current school building was built in 1911. There are 75 students at the school.

But solar panels are expensive. How could a small school like Chewton afford this? Using crowd funding, many community groups and local businesses donated money for the solar panel project.

In 2015, the solar panels were installed. Now, most of the energy the school is using is clean energy. And, this fits perfectly with the school values of being sustainable and looking after the environment.

Solar panels placed on the roof ensure that energy is produced during the time when it's most needed – in the morning through to the early afternoon.

Saving energy and money

As well as saving energy, which is good for the environment, the use of solar power has another big benefit. It saves money. The school no longer has a big electricity bill to pay. The money saved helps to pay for environmentally-friendly projects that benefit the whole town. For example, the school has undertaken a local bush regeneration project, and it has a community garden and cooking program.

Students are involved in programs that help the community, such as the community garden and the bush regeneration program.

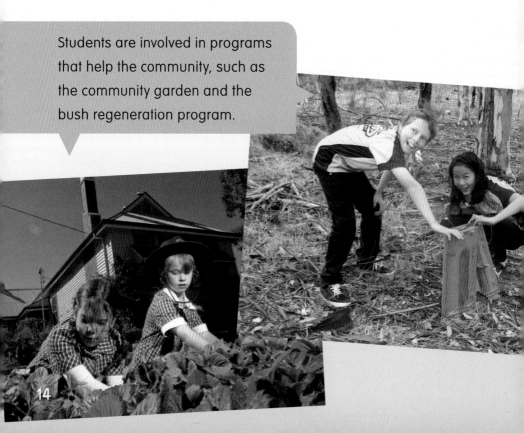

A cubby for the playground that has been built from recycled materials

Other major things Chewton PS has done to reduce energy use:
- Replaced all the light globes with energy-efficient globes
- Topped up ceiling insulation
- Capped chimneys to stop losing lots of heat
- Draft-proofed all doors
- Adopted green purchasing policy: all new appliances must have the best star rating possible
- Started a "Switch off" program: turning off all lights not in use
- Encouraged "winter warmer" days: students and staff wear jumpers before a heater can be turned on
- Installed automatic switch-off timers on electrical appliances and sensor lights

Chapter 3

Renewable energy – Hope for Haiti

In 2010, an earthquake devastated the country of Haiti, which is in the Caribbean, off the coast of North America. Thousands of people were killed and injured and many more lost their homes as buildings everywhere collapsed. People were left without electricity and without the ability to communicate with the outside world.

The Haitian people and volunteers from around the world struggled to provide medical care, food and shelter to the injured and displaced.

Much of the capital city Port-au-Prince was destroyed by the earthquake in 2010.

A solar panel charges outside a tent in a makeshift camp

Haiti had long been dependent on non-renewable energy resources, which had a destructive impact on the environment. Over time, the land had been stripped of its forests and natural resources.

However, after the 2010 earthquake, renewable energy resources played a surprising role in the recovery process. Solar energy provided an immediate source of energy. Solar-powered street lights provided the only practical light source. Relief workers used solar-powered mobile phones to communicate with each other. And in hospitals, solar panels delivered electricity.

The short-term success of solar energy encouraged the Haitian people to try new environmentally friendly tools to accomplish everyday tasks.

Solar torches

Relief workers were able to work at night using solar torches – a safe and reliable alternative to dangerous kerosene lanterns or candles. And for the millions of families living in tent cities, these solar torches offered a sense of comfort and safety.

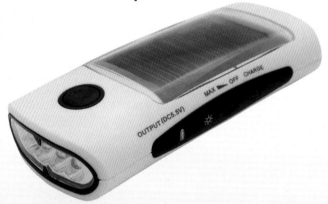

Clean water

Solar disinfection can prevent waterborne parasites and diseases that had plagued Haitians before and after the earthquake. This method works by filling a plastic bottle with the contaminated water and placing it in the sun for about five hours. The sun's rays burn away any bacteria that exist.

Solar cooking

Solar cooking is considered the long-term green alternative to charcoal, the non-renewable fuel source that Haiti has long been dependent on for cooking. Solar cooking works by using focused sunlight to heat food and boil water. This will allow the land to recover and the forests to grow again.

The success of simple, effective and, best of all, unlimited renewable energy in Haiti offers hope to people. They may be poor in material possessions but they are rich in spirit and ever more aware of the potential of natural resources to improve their lives.

Box solar cookers are easy to make. A cooking pot covered in plastic is placed in front of the panels.

Chapter 4

New York's Lowline Park

Using mirrors to redirect natural sunlight from the surface, New York City in the United States plans to create the world's first underground park. Solar energy will enable plants to grow underground. In a few years, people will be able to walk into what was once an old Manhattan tram tunnel to find it filled with flowers and plants from around the world.

The Lowline Lab, New York City, was set up to test how the plants would grow underground.

Aerial view of New York City. The Lowline will provide New York's residents with more green space.

Plants need sunlight, so how will they grow?

The park, which is called the Lowline, will use mirrors at street level to collect light. These mirrors swivel and follow the sun as it moves across the sky. The sunlight is collected and concentrated so that it is 30 times stronger than the sunlight on the street. It is then distributed in clear tubes that will zigzag across the roof of the garden. Bathed in this sunlight, plants are able to grow.

The kinds of plants have been carefully chosen to ensure that they will grow in this underground environment.

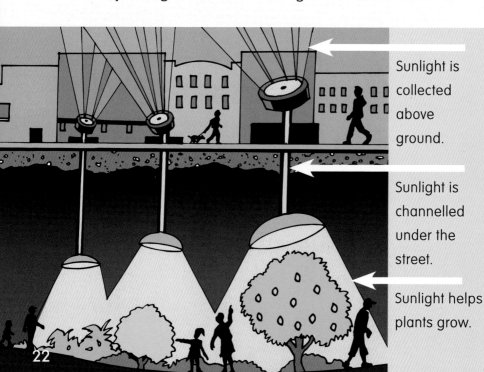

Sunlight is collected above ground.

Sunlight is channelled under the street.

Sunlight helps plants grow.

The Lowline Lab in New York City was open to the public from October 2015 to February 2017. Over 100 different varieties of plants were grown in the Lab.

There is still a lot of experimental work to be done and many problems to solve before the park opens in 2021. But if this park succeeds, other cities will be able to build their own underground parks. As well as being a beautiful green area for people to enjoy all year around, this underground park might become a place where all sorts of food crops could be grown in the city.

Chapter 5 | Energy in the future

People are continuing to explore new ideas that use clean, renewable energy. Most cars run by burning fuel and they emit dangerous gases into the air. However, there are cars that use different energy sources.

Electric cars

Electric cars use electricity that is stored in a battery to run the motor. These cars need to be plugged into a power source to recharge the battery. Often, the electricity used to charge the car is made by burning fossil fuels, which affects the environment. But electric cars do not emit gases, which is good news for the environment.

Electric cars are more expensive than cars that use gas. They are also very heavy because of the weight of the battery. But designs are improving and many experts believe that in the future, most cars will be electric and that cars will be charged using electricity made from renewable energy.

Hybrid cars

Hybrid cars use both electricity and gas. When the car is on flat ground at lower speeds, the electric motor is used to save gas. When more power or speed is needed, the engine converts to using gas.

These two models of solar cars were developed for solar power challenges.

Solar cars

Solar cars run by using energy directly from the sun. Large PV (photo voltaic) cells on top of the car collect energy from the sun to make the motor work. Solar cars do not emit gases and don't need to be plugged in to charge. Presently, solar cars are only at the experimental stage and are not suitable for driving on the road.

The future of flight

An aeroplane recently flew around the world using no fuel – just the power of the sun!

This solar aeroplane travelled over 40,000 kilometres at an average speed of 80 kilometres an hour. The small plane weighs the same as a car, but has large wings packed with PV cells. Many people did not believe that this flight was possible but it happened. Maybe one day we will all be travelling in solar-powered aeroplanes!

A solar-powered aeroplane

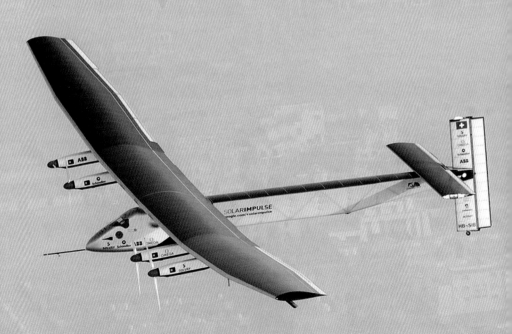

Solar-powered phone chargers

Green gadgets

Designers and inventors are coming up with ideas for products that use renewable energy sources such as wind, sun and water to reduce the amount of electricity generated by burning fossil fuels. Scientists and designers are continuing to develop new technologies using renewable energy as a power source.

We can all become more aware of saving power whenever possible. By doing this, you too can help make our world a cleaner, more energy-efficient place.

Conclusion

We need energy to do many of the things we take for granted. But we must also look after our planet. More and more people around the world are using renewable energy sources. They are aware that using fossil fuels damages our planet. Many people install solar panels in their homes because it is a cheaper form of energy. They save money and help save the planet.

It is no longer wise to use fossil fuels as our main energy source. Using the sun, the wind and the flow of water and heat from underground are clean ways to produce energy and power our world. And, best of all, these resources will never run out.

Index